VICTORIAN HOUSE DESIGNS

IN AUTHENTIC FULL COLOR

75 Plates from the "Scientific American—
Architects and Builders Edition,"
1885–1894

Edited by
Blanche Cirker

DOVER PUBLICATIONS, INC.
Mineola, New York

Copyright

Copyright © 1996 by Dover Publications, Inc.
All rights reserved under Pan American and International Copyright Conventions.

Published in Canada by General Publishing Company, Ltd., 30 Lesmill Road, Don Mills,
Toronto, Ontario.
Published in the United Kingdom by Constable and Company, Ltd., 3 The Lanchesters,
162–164 Fulham Palace Road, London W6 9ER.

Bibliographical Note

*Victorian House Designs in Authentic Full Color: 75 Plates from the "Scientific American—
Architects and Builders Edition," 1885–1894* is a new work, first published by Dover
Publications, Inc., in 1996.

Library of Congress Cataloging-in-Publication Data

Victorian house designs in authentic full color : 75 plates from the Scientific American—
    architects and builders edition, 1885–1894 / edited by Blanche Cirker.
        p.   cm.
    Includes indexes.
    ISBN 0-486-29438-2 (pbk.)
    1. Architecture, Victorian—United States—Designs and plans. 2. Architecture,
Domestic—United States—Designs and Plans. I. Cirker, Blanche.
NA7206.V54   1996
728'.37'0222—dc21   96-47807
                                                                              CIP

Manufactured in the United States of America
Dover Publications, Inc., 31 East 2nd Street, Mineola, N.Y. 11501

Publisher's Note

Between 1885 and 1905, Munn & Co., New York, issued a periodical variously titled *Scientific American—Architects and Builders Edition* (November 1885–December 1894), *Scientific American Building Edition* (January 1895–December 1901) and *Scientific American Building Monthly* (January 1902–June 1905). Issues were accompanied by lithographic plates illustrating various structures. It is a selection made from these plates that comprises the present work.

By the end of the 1870s, a number of styles had dominated American architecture: Colonial, Federal, Greek Revival, Italianate, Gothic Revival, Second Empire, Neo-Grec, Carpenter's Gothic and Stick Style. In 1876, at the British Pavilion of the 1876 Centennial Exposition in Philadelphia, a new style, the so-called Queen Anne, was introduced and found immediate favor. The name of the style is strange, for there is nothing in it of the architectural styles practiced during the reign of Queen Anne (1702–14). Queen Anne houses are distinguished by a "picturesque" use of towers, turrets, gables, porches, chimneys and other elements to produce a striking silhouette. They also incorporate unstinting decoration, heavy use of polychromy and a variety of surfaces (wood, stone, brick, shingle). Most of the houses illustrated here are Queen Anne in style.

Also included are houses in other styles that marked the eighties and nineties: The Shingle Style (e.g., pp. 5, 27, 47, 59, 60), in which most surfaces are covered with shingles (frequently unpainted), including siding and gables. The Moorish style (p. 11) features tile decoration, "horseshoe" windows and arches; the Romanesque Revival (p. 48) is characterized by heavy massing and the use of arches. The Colonial Revival, also represented (pp. 56, 64, 65, 68, 74), frequently reveals the awkwardness created by the discrepancy between the symmetry that marks Georgian architecture and the asymmetrical massing favored during the seventies and eighties.

Worthy of special note is the fluidity of space on the main floors of many of the plans shown here, pocket doors allowing space to be expanded or contracted. The plan shown on page 8, for example, reveals the potential of a vista of over 35 feet extending from the reception room through the library. The size and the location of the hall makes it possible to use the entire ground floor, with the exception of the kitchen wing, to be opened into one space for entertaining. Such arrangements are uniquely American, and are only rarely to be found in European houses of the period.

SIDE ELEVATION.

FRONT ELEVATION.

A Village Residence.

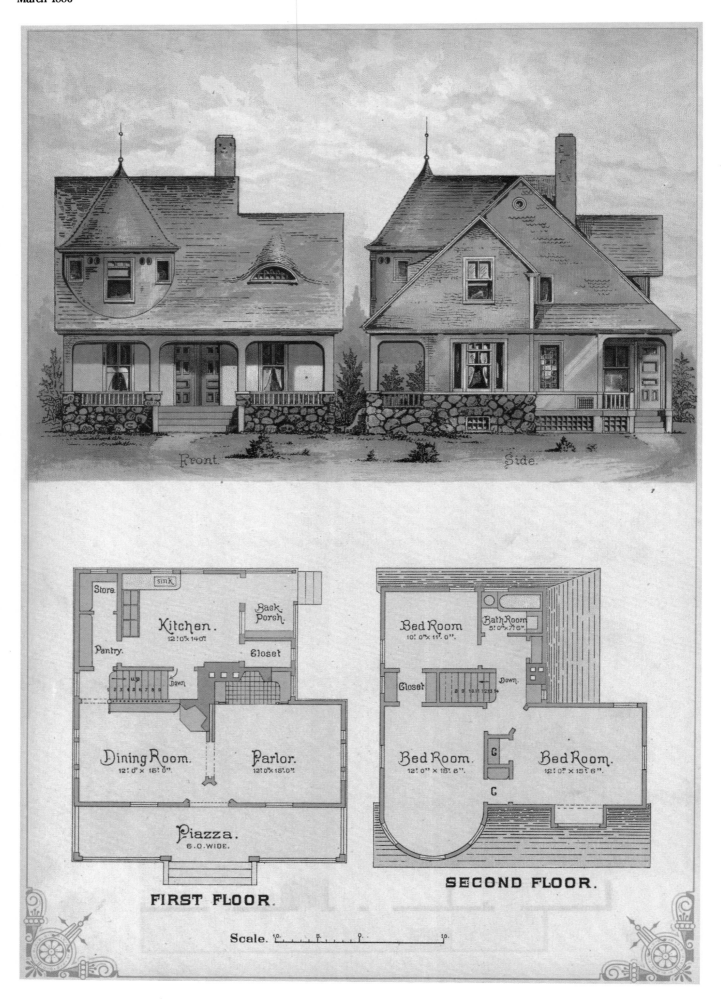

Front.   Side.

FIRST FLOOR.

Store.   sink   Back Porch.

Kitchen.
12' 0" x 14' 0".

Pantry.   Closet.

up   Down

Dining Room.   Parlor.
12' 0" x 16' 0".   12' 0" x 15' 0".

Piazza.
6. 0. WIDE.

SECOND FLOOR.

Bed Room   Bath Room
10' 0" x 11' 0".   5' 0" x 7' 6".

Closet   Down

Bed Room   C   Bed Room.
12' 0" x 16' 6".   12' 0" x 15' 6".

C

Scale.

SUPPLEMENT TO THE SCIENTIFIC AMERICAN-ARCHITECTS AND BUILDERS EDITION - JUNE 1886.

A HOUSE AT ORANGE. N.J.

JOSEPH A. STARK, ARCHITECT, NEW YORK.

A COTTAGE AT MONMOUTH BEACH, N.J. T.A. ROBERTS & SON, ARCHITECTS, NEWARK, N.J.

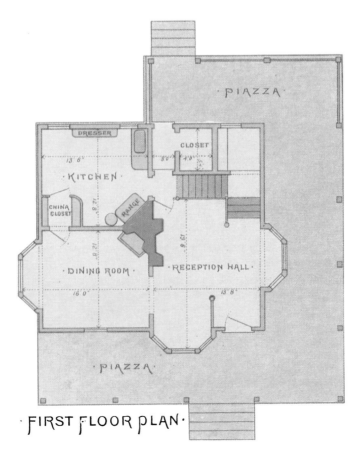

FIRST FLOOR PLAN

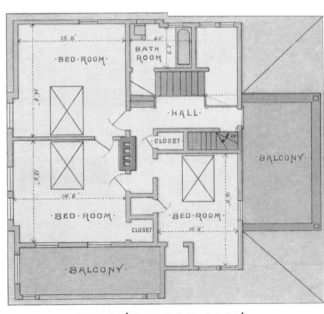

SECOND FLOOR PLAN

A DWELLING AT FLATBUSH, N.Y. H.L.HARRIS, ARCHITECT, N.Y.

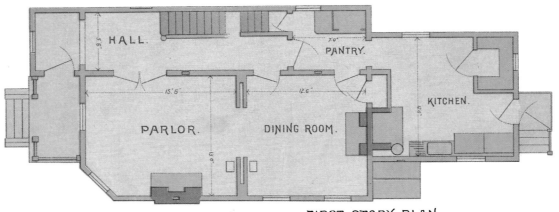

FIRST STORY PLAN.

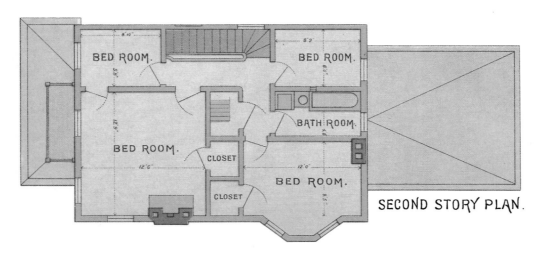

SECOND STORY PLAN.

A COUNTRY RESIDENCE AT YONKERS, N.Y.   H.S. RAPELYE ARCHITECT, M™ VERNON N.Y.

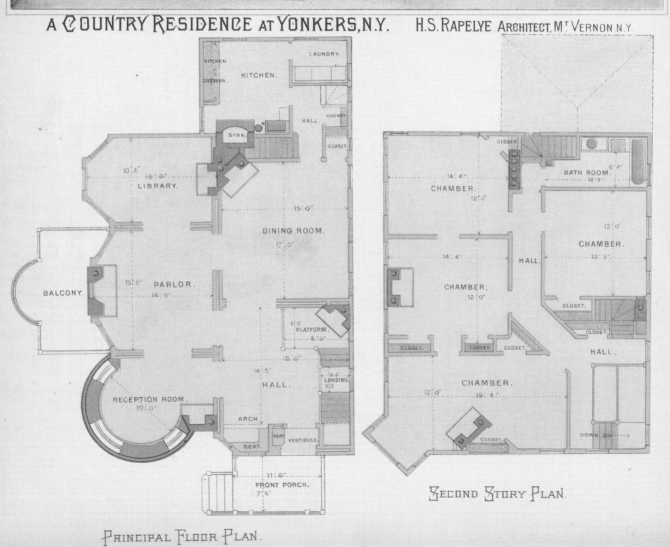

PRINCIPAL FLOOR PLAN.

SECOND STORY PLAN.

A COTTAGE AT BLOCK ISLAND, R.I. CHAS. E. MILLER, ARCHITECT, NEW YORK.

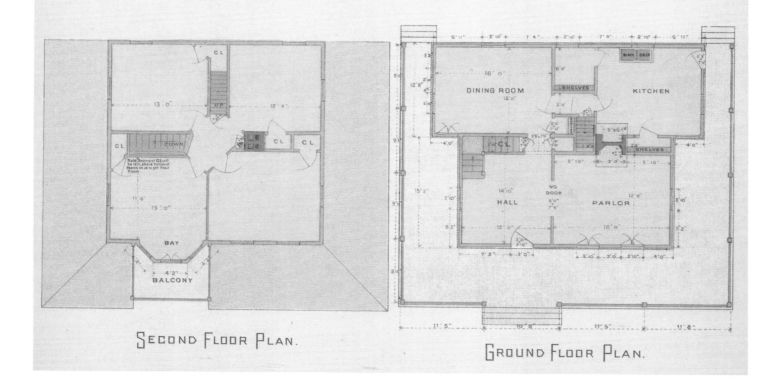

SECOND FLOOR PLAN.

GROUND FLOOR PLAN.

AN $1800 DWELLING · DESIGNED BY FRANK D. NICHOLS, BRIDGEPORT, CONN.

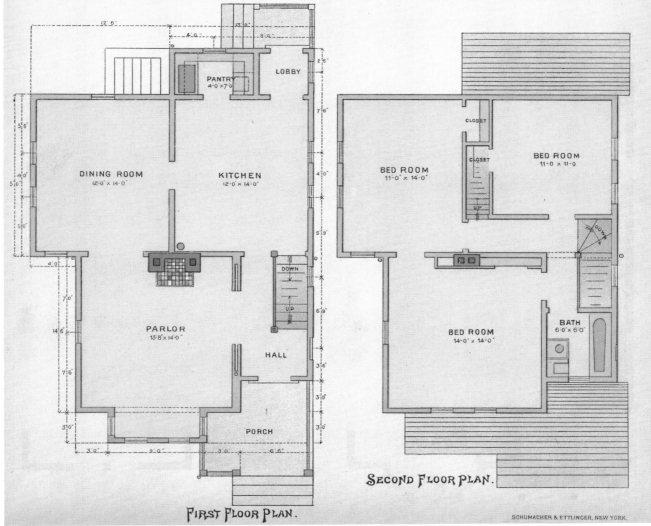

FIRST FLOOR PLAN.

SECOND FLOOR PLAN.

A SWISS COTTAGE AT WEST NEW BRIGHTON, N.Y.
D. W. KING, ARCHITECT, N.Y.

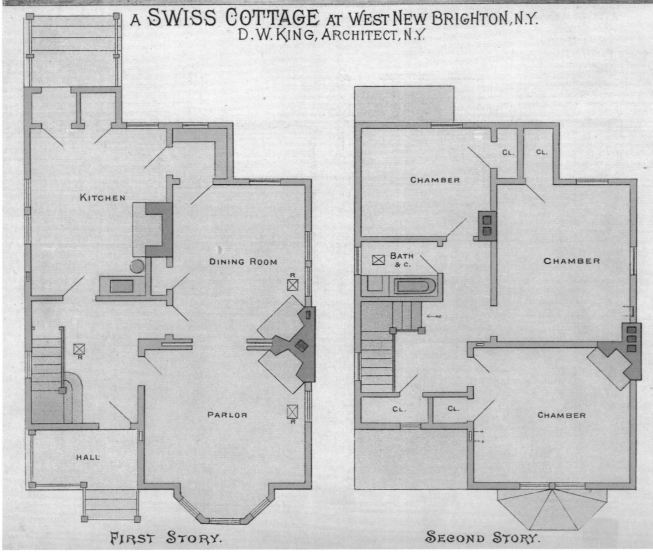

FIRST STORY.   SECOND STORY.

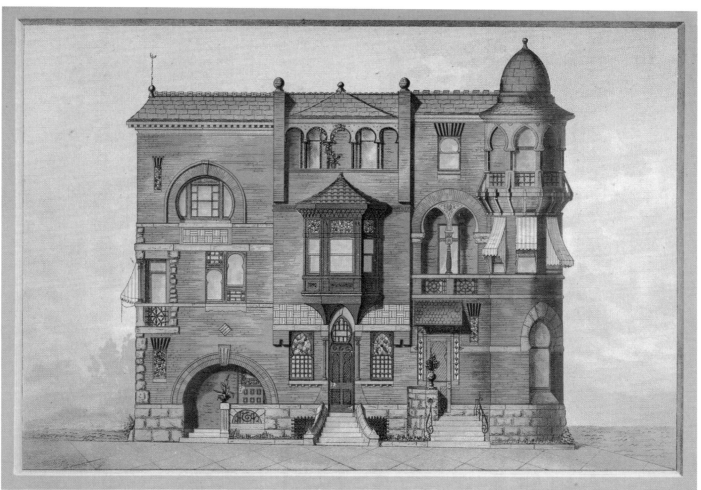

· A BLOCK OF BRICK DWELLINGS OF MODERATE COST ·   W. CLAUDE FREDERIC, Architect, Baltimore, Md.

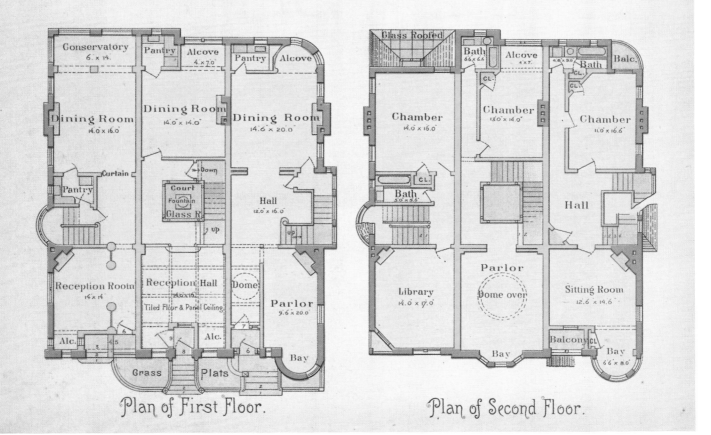

Plan of First Floor.

Plan of Second Floor.

St James' Rectory, Fordham, N.Y.   Edward A. Sargent, Architect, New York.

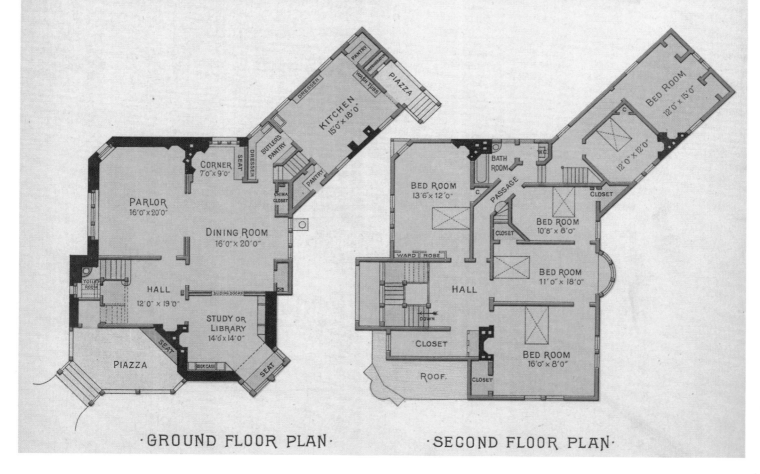

· GROUND FLOOR PLAN ·   · SECOND FLOOR PLAN ·

THE FARRAGUT CLUB HOUSE, CHICAGO. ROB. RAE, Jʀ. Architect.

A Two Thousand Six Hundred *Dollar* Cottage. GEORGE W. CADY, ARCHITECT.

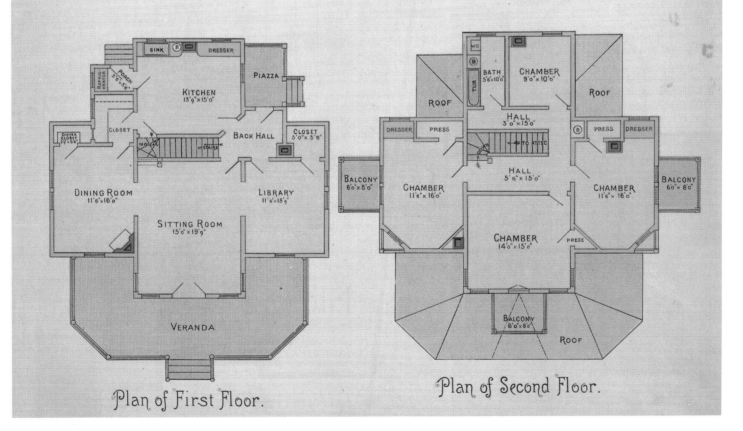

Plan of First Floor.

Plan of Second Floor.

RESIDENCE OF F.W. COOLBAUGH, ESQ. EAST ORANGE N.J.   GEORGE COOKE, ARCHITECT.

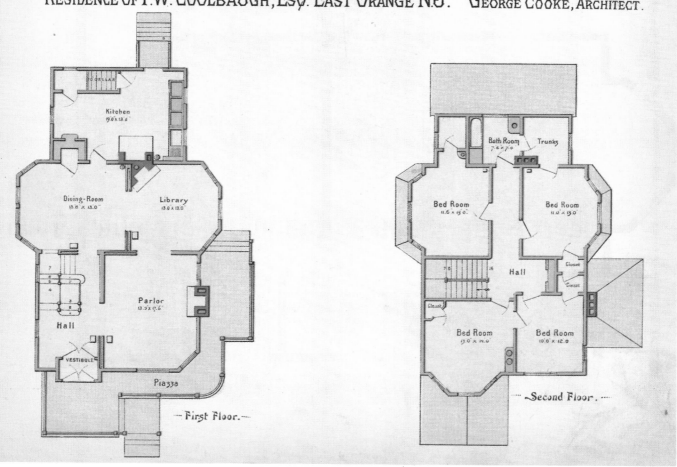

First Floor.

Second Floor.

A COTTAGE OF MODERATE COST INTENDED FOR FUTURE ENLARGEMENT.

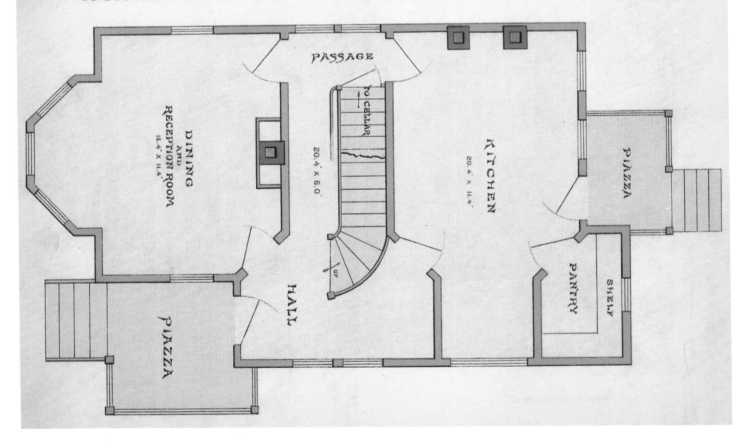

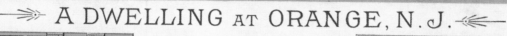

A DWELLING AT ORANGE, N.J.

Plan of First Floor.

Plan of Second Floor.

· A · Twelve · Hundred · Dollar · Cottage ·

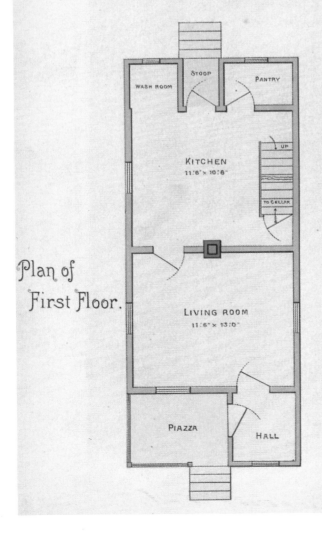

Plan of
First Floor.

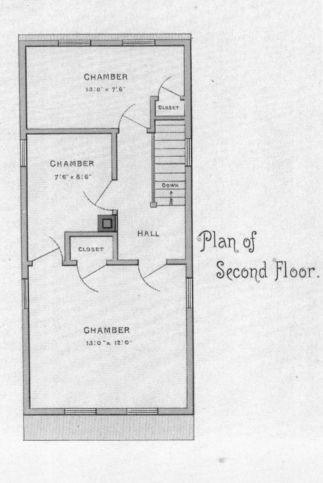

Plan of
Second Floor.

A·Residence·Costing·Five·Thousand·Dollars·

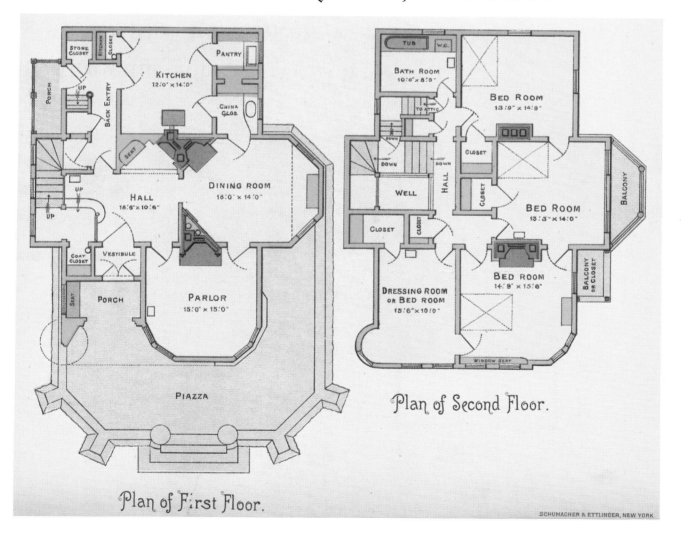

Plan of First Floor.

Plan of Second Floor.

A·Residence·in·Kansas·City;·Mo·.

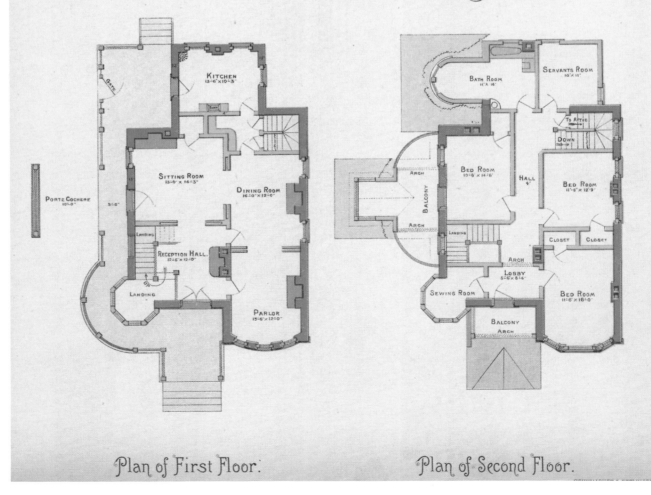

Plan of First Floor.   Plan of Second Floor.

A Southern Residence of Moderate Cost.

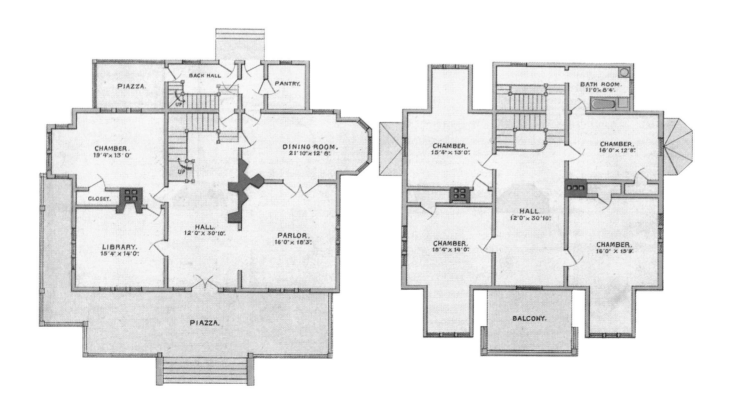

Plan of First Floor.   Plan of Second Floor.

A Residence of Moderate Cost.

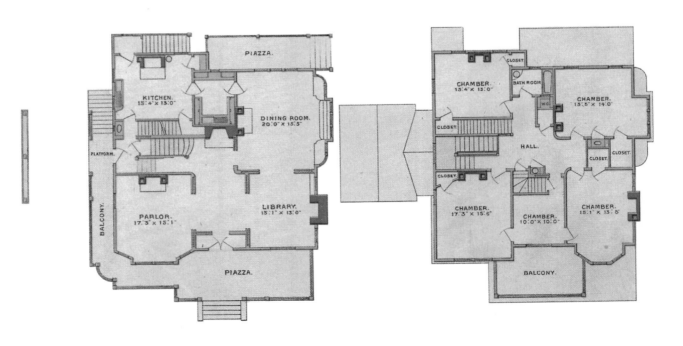

Plan of First Floor.   Plan of Second Floor.

A Country Store and Flat.

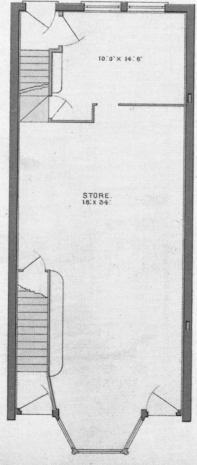

Plan of First Floor.

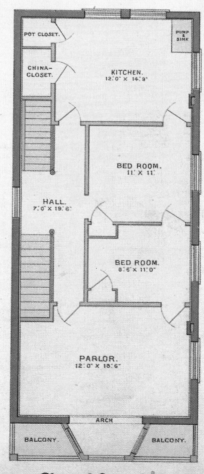

Plan of Second Floor.

⋙ City Frame Houses of Moderate Cost. ⋘

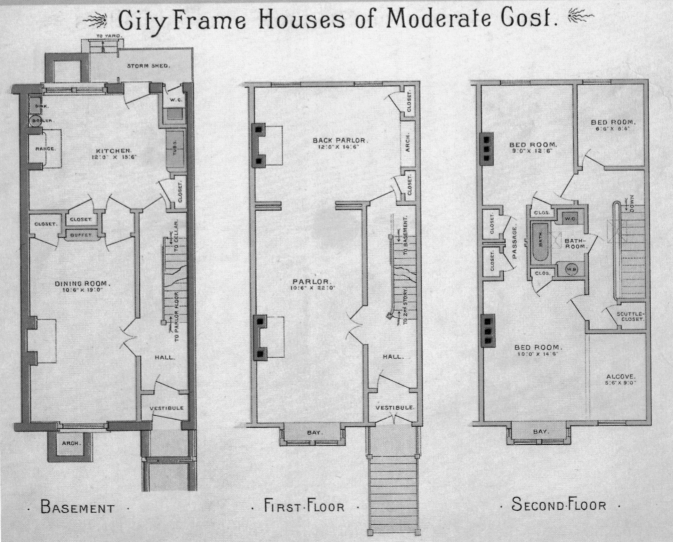

· BASEMENT ·   · FIRST·FLOOR ·   · SECOND·FLOOR ·

A Dwelling for *Two* ~~Five~~ Thousand Five Hundred Dollars.

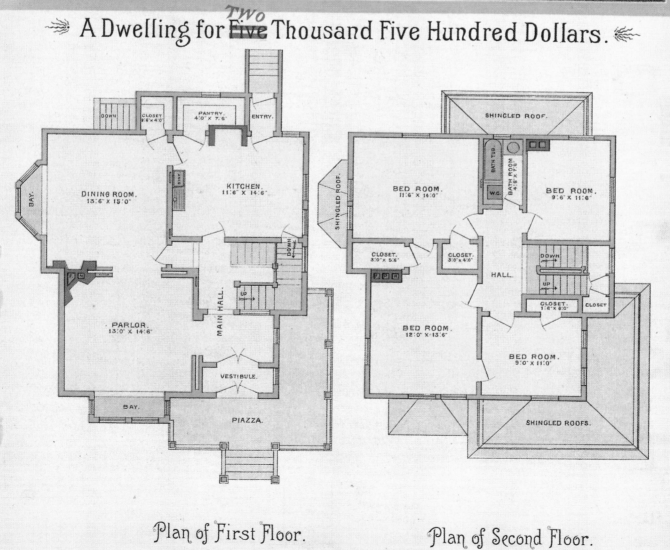

Plan of First Floor.   Plan of Second Floor.

✳ A SUBURBAN RESIDENCE ✳

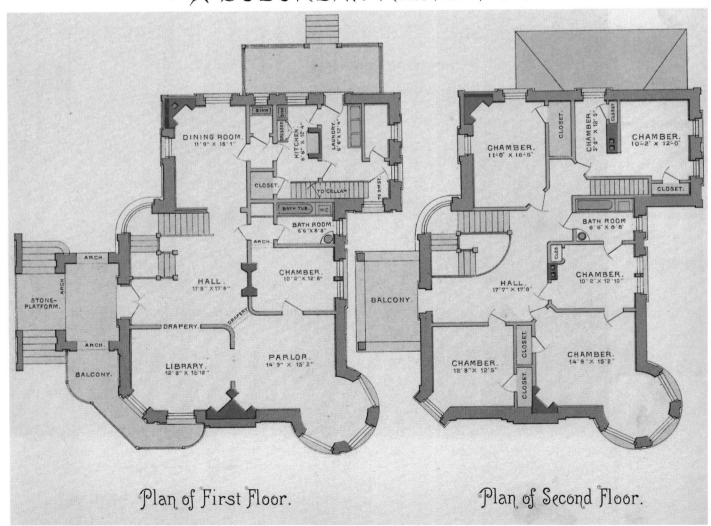

Plan of First Floor.   Plan of Second Floor.

✳ A DWELLING OF MODERATE COST ✳

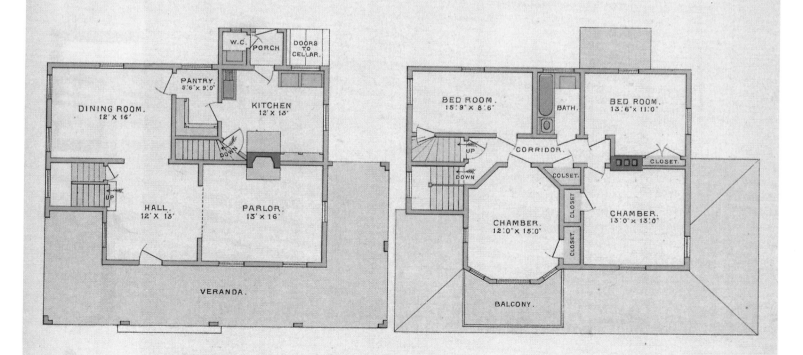

Plan of First Floor.   Plan of Second Floor.

A Residence in Michigan.

Plan of First Floor.

Plan of Second Floor.

✺ Two Dwellings at Orange, N. J. ✺

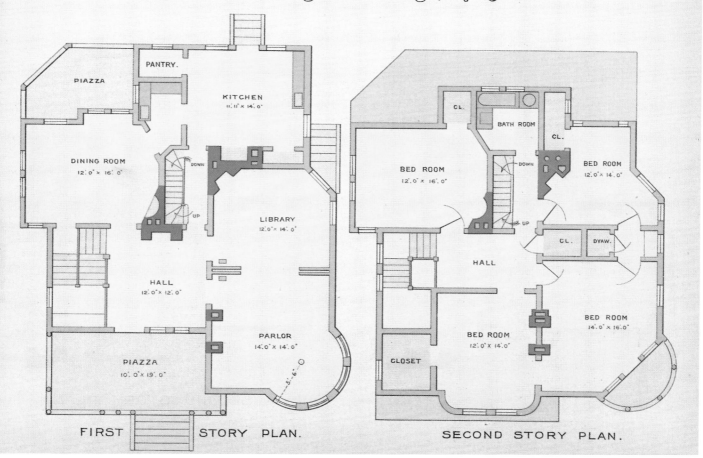

PIAZZA

PANTRY.

KITCHEN
11'. 11" x 14'. 0"

DINING ROOM
12'. 0" x 16'. 0"

DOWN

UP

LIBRARY
12'. 0" x 14'. 0"

HALL
12'. 0" x 12'. 0"

PARLOR
14'. 0" x 14'. 0"

PIAZZA
10'. 0" x 19'. 0"

5'. 6"

FIRST   STORY PLAN.

CL.

BATH ROOM

CL.

BED ROOM
12'. 0" x 16'. 0"

DOWN

BED ROOM
12'. 0" x 14'. 0"

CL.   DYAW.

HALL

UP

BED ROOM
14'. 0" x 16'. 0"

BED ROOM
12'. 0" x 14'. 0"

CLOSET

SECOND STORY PLAN.

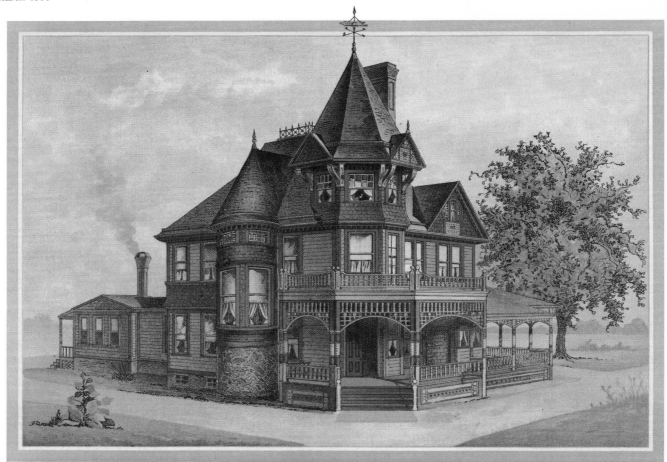

A Suburban Residence.

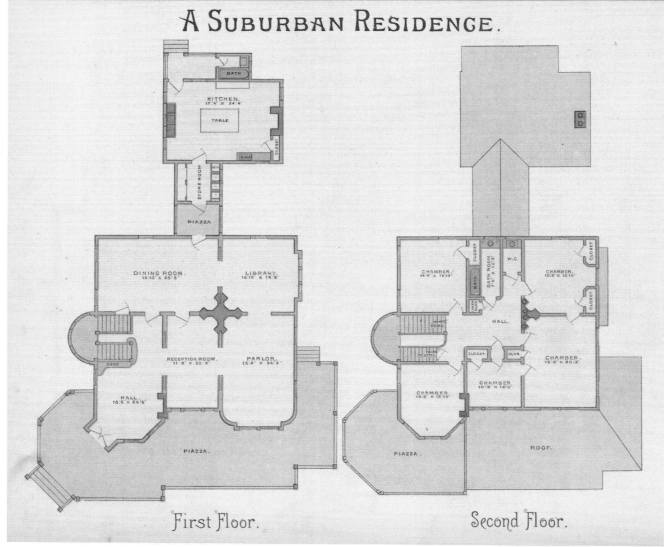

First Floor.   Second Floor.

A COTTAGE OF MODERATE COST.

· A RESIDENCE at TUXEDO PARK, N.J ·

↤ A Suburban Dwelling. ↦

A Dwelling at Glen Ridge, N.J.

⤙ A Fire Engine House of Moderate Cost ⤚

A Suburban Dwelling of Moderate Cost.

COTTAGES FOR FIFTEEN HUNDRED DOLLARS

A SUBURBAN CLUB HOUSE.

A DWELLING FOR FIVE THOUSAND DOLLARS.

FIRST FLOOR PLAN.

SECOND FLOOR PLAN.

A Dwelling of Moderate Cost

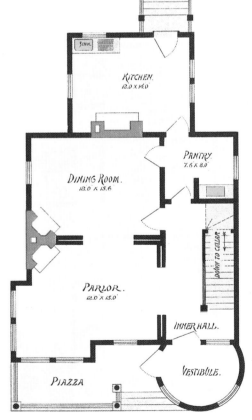

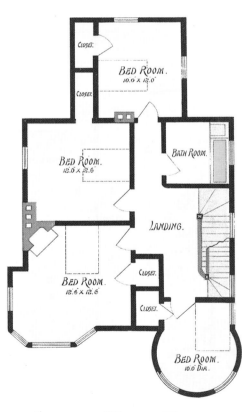

First Floor Plan.

Second Floor Plan.

RESIDENCE of C·W·MILLER Esq· STATEN ISLAND.

RESIDENCE of E·BRIDGEMAN Esq· STATEN ISLAND.

A COTTAGE FOR FIFTEEN HUNDRED DOLLARS.

A COTTAGE FOR ONE THOUSAND DOLLARS.

A RESIDENCE ON LONG ISLAND.

FIRST STORY PLAN.

SECOND STORY PLAN.

A COTTAGE AT BUFFALO, N.Y.

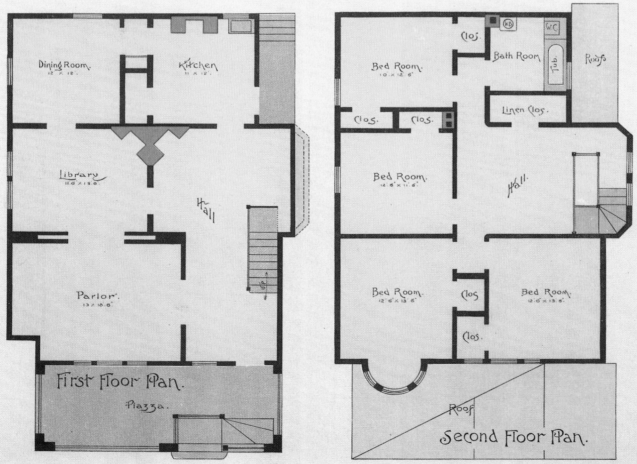

First Floor Plan.

Dining Room. 12 x 12.

Kitchen 11 x 12.

Library 11.0 x 13.0.

Hall

Parlor. 13 x 18.6.

Piazza.

Second Floor Plan.

Clos.

Bath Room

Tub.

W.C.

Roofs

Bed Room. 10 x 12.6.

Clos.   Clos.

Linen Clos.

Bed Room. 12.6 x 11.6.

Hall.

Bed Room. 12.6 x 13.6.

Clos

Clos.

Bed Room. 12.6 x 13.6.

Roof

· A RESIDENCE AT MONTCLAIR ·

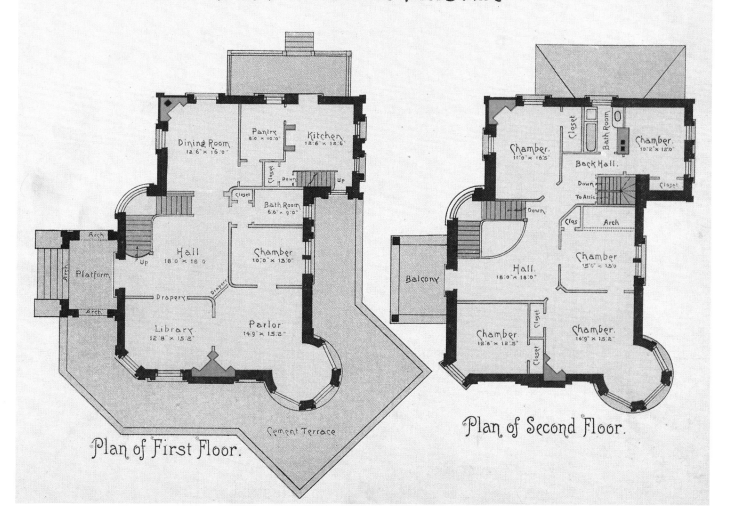

Plan of First Floor.

Plan of Second Floor.

RESIDENCE OF HENRY R. TOWNE ESQ. Stamford Conn.

First Floor.

Second Floor.

· A LONG ISLAND RESIDENCE ·

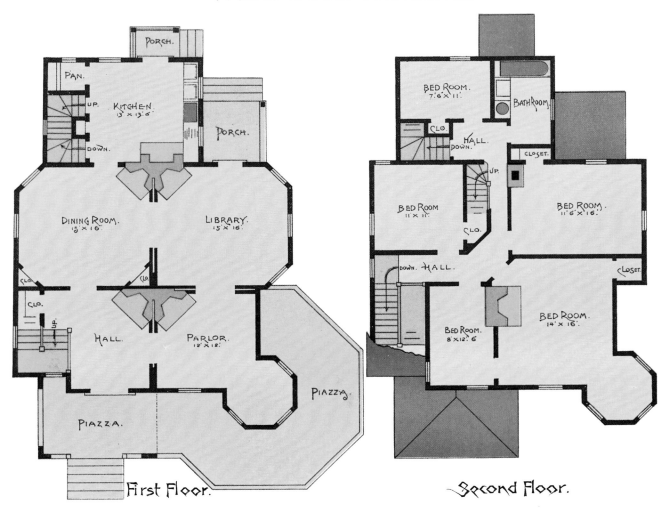

First Floor.

Second Floor.

A Residence on Riverside Park, New York.

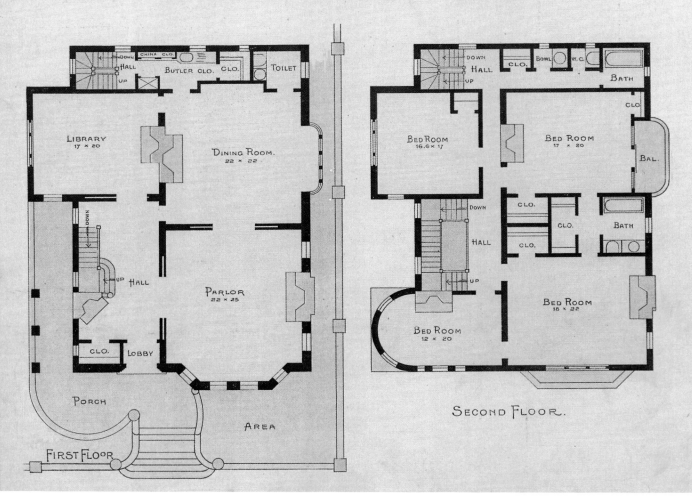

A Residence at Mount Vernon, N.Y.

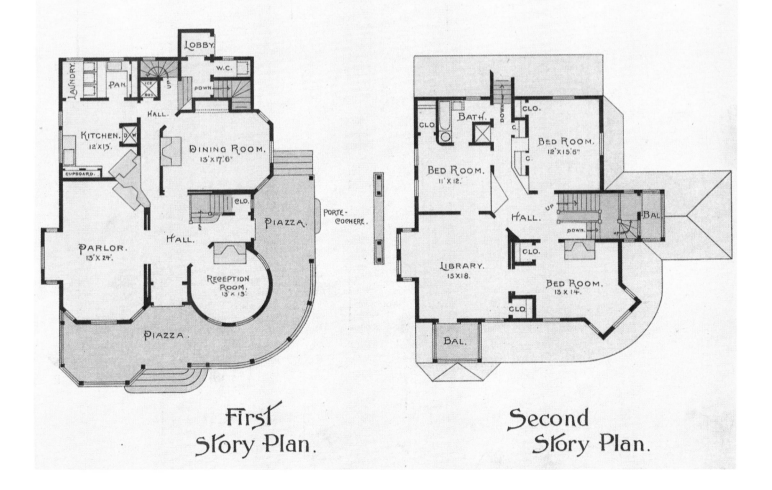

First
Story Plan.

Second
Story Plan.

A Residence at Auburn Park, Chicago.

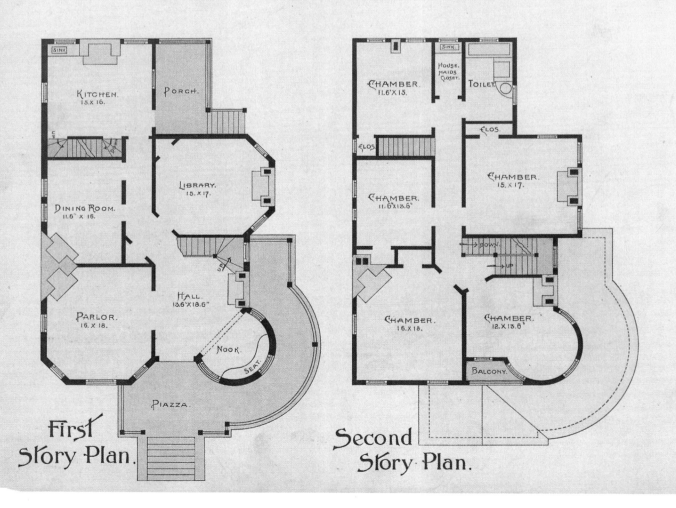

First Story Plan.

Second Story Plan.

A Residence At Bridgeport Conn.

KITCHEN. 14'X17'

PAN.

BUTLER CLO.

LOBBY.

UP HALL

DOWN.

DINING ROOM 14'X17'.

CLO.   TOILET.

HALL

LIBRARY 14'X18'.

CLO.   LOBBY

PARLOR 15'X15'.

PLATFORM.

BATH ROOM.

C.

CLO.

BED ROOM 14'X17'

HALL.

BED ROOM 14'X17'

DOWN.

CLO.   HALL.   CLO.

CLO.

BED ROOM 14'X18'.

CLO.   CLO.

CLO.

DRESSING ROOM 10'X16'.

BED ROOM 15'X15'6".

SEGOND FLOOR.

A Residence At Bridgeport, Conn.

First Floor.

Second Floor.

BRICK DWELLINGS OF MODERATE COST.

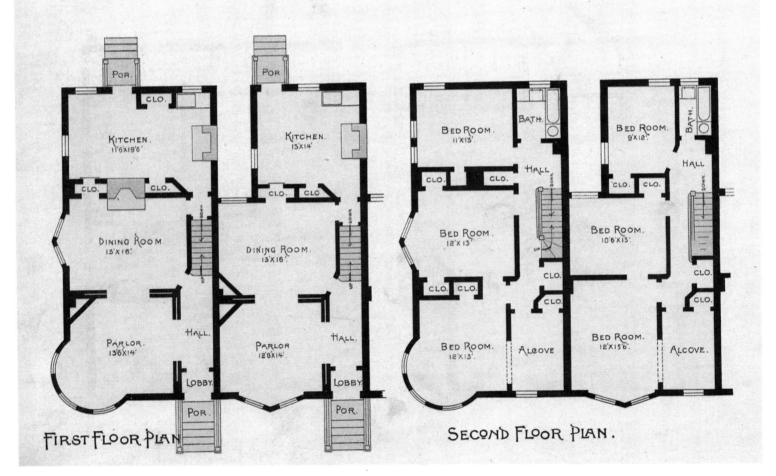

FIRST FLOOR PLAN.   SECOND FLOOR PLAN.

A RESIDENCE ON RIVERSIDE PARK, NEW YORK.

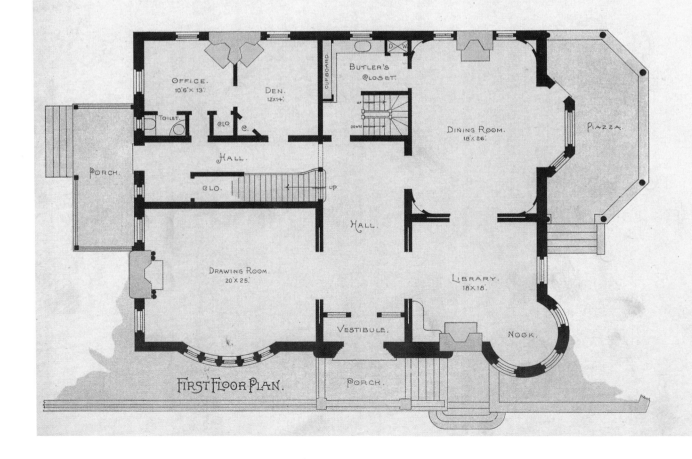

FIRST FLOOR PLAN.

A SUBURBAN DWELLING.

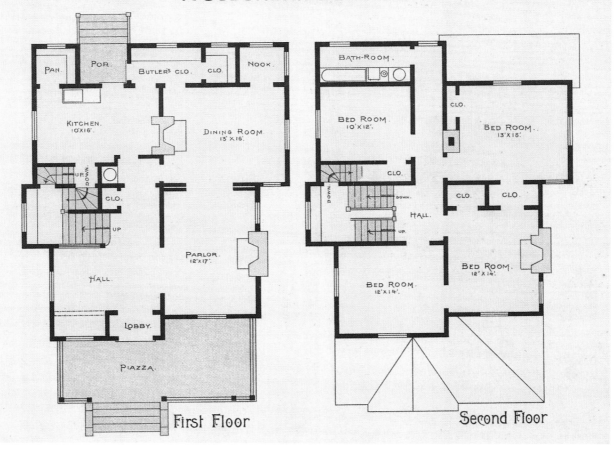

First Floor

Second Floor

A RESIDENCE, FORDHAM HEIGHTS, N.Y.

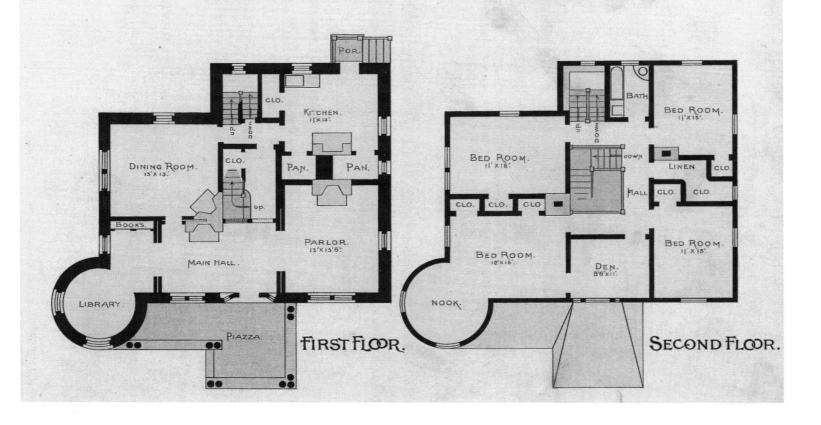

FIRST FLOOR.

SECOND FLOOR.

A RESIDENCE AT LARCHMONT MANOR.

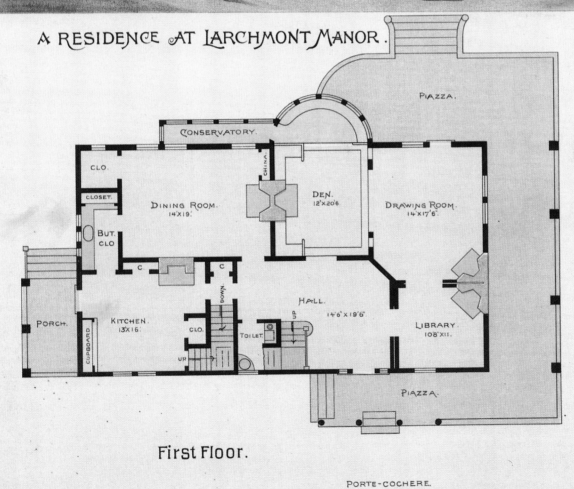

First Floor.

PORTE-COCHERE.

A TWENTY FIVE HUNDRED DOLLAR HOUSE.

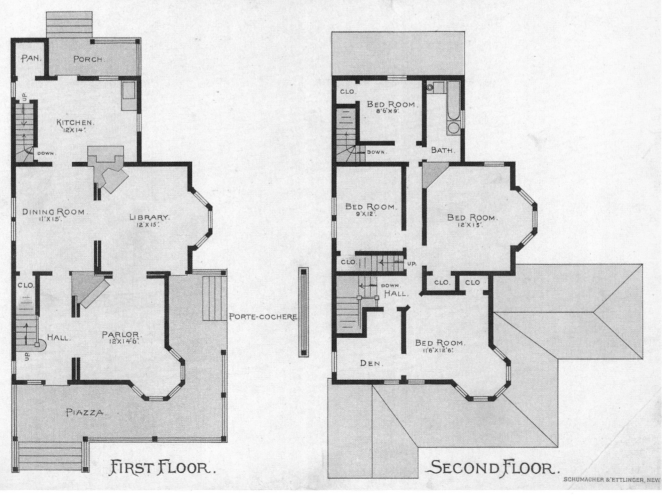

FIRST FLOOR.

SECOND FLOOR.

A Cottage in Maine.- Cost.$900.

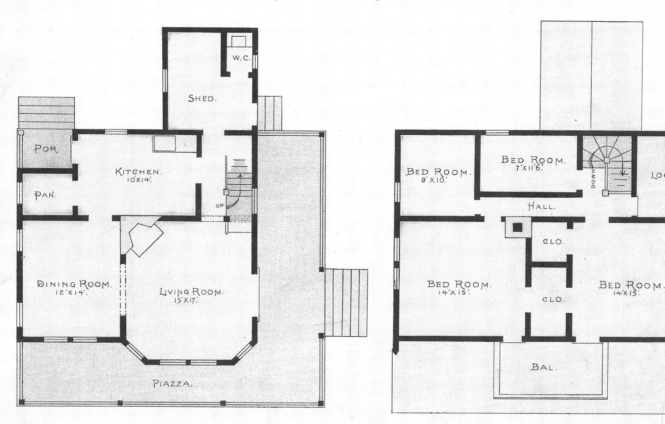

FIRST FLOOR.   SECOND FLOOR.

A Cottage at New Rochelle.

FIRST FLOOR.   SECOND FLOOR.

A RESIDENCE AT BRIDGEPORT, CONN.

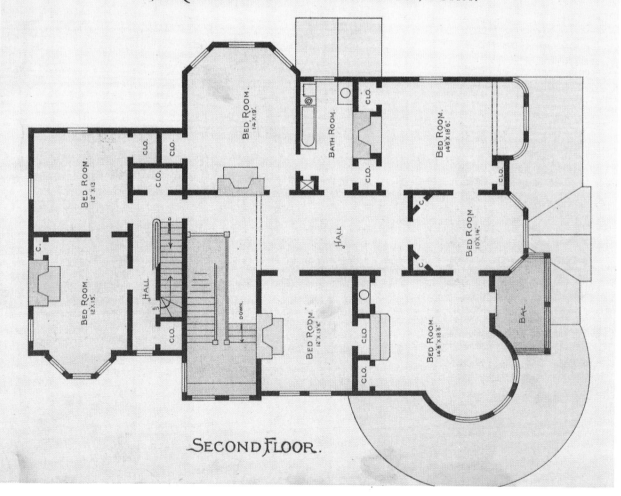

SECOND FLOOR.

A COTTAGE NEAR PORTLAND, MAINE.

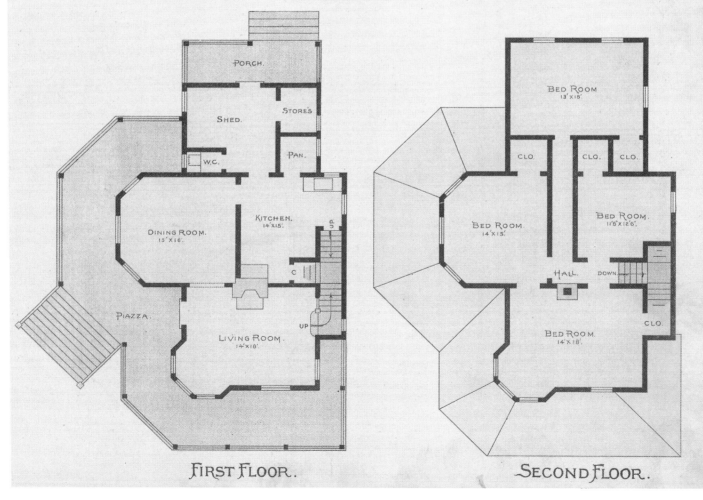

FIRST FLOOR.   SECOND FLOOR.

A RESIDENCE IN BROOKLYN, N.Y.

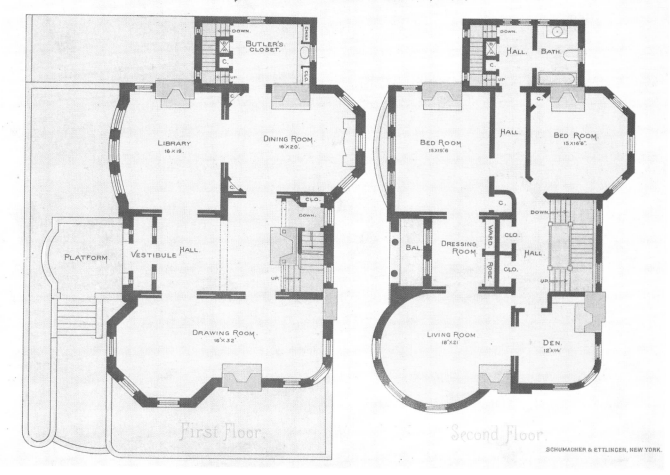

First Floor.

Second Floor.

SCHUMACHER & ETTLINGER, NEW YORK.

A HOUSE AT MONTCLAIR, N.J.

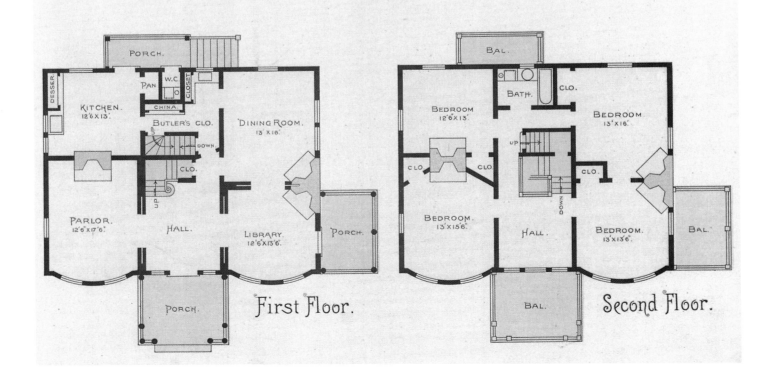

First Floor.

Second Floor.

A Colonial Residence.

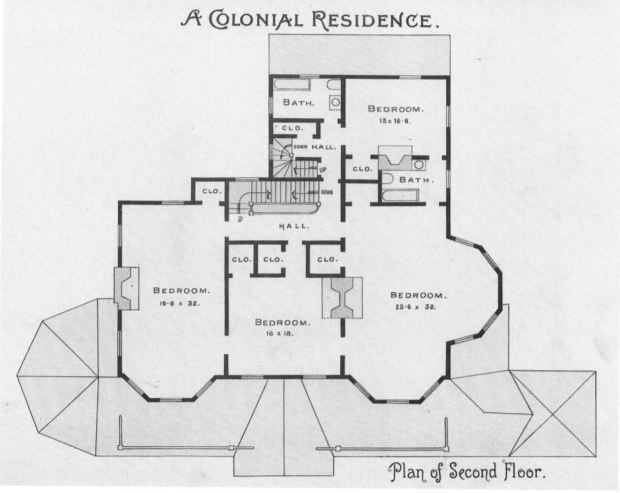

BATH.

CLO.

BEDROOM.
13 x 16·6

DOWN HALL.

UP

CLO.

DOWN

BATH.

CLO.

CLO.   CLO.   CLO.

HALL.

BEDROOM.
16·6 x 32.

BEDROOM.
25·6 x 32.

BEDROOM.
16 x 18.

Plan of Second Floor.

CITY RESIDENCES, NEW YORK.

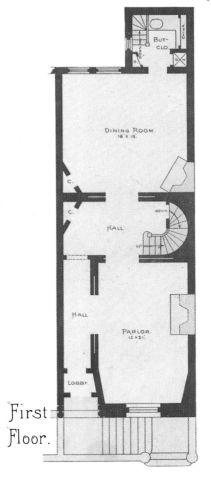

First Floor.

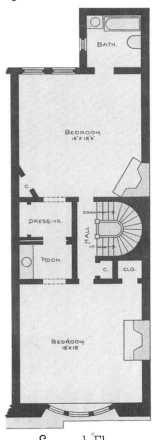

Second Floor.

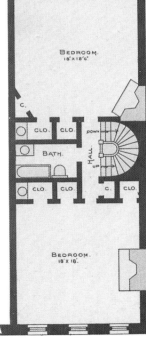

Third Floor.

A DWELLING AT WARBERTH PARK, PA.

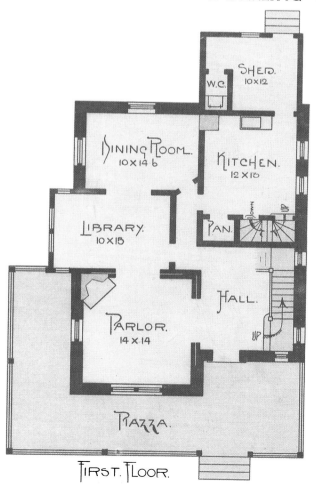

FIRST FLOOR.

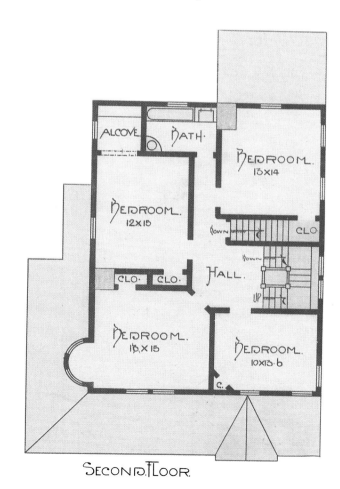

SECOND FLOOR.

A RESIDENCE AT BRIDGEPORT, CONN.

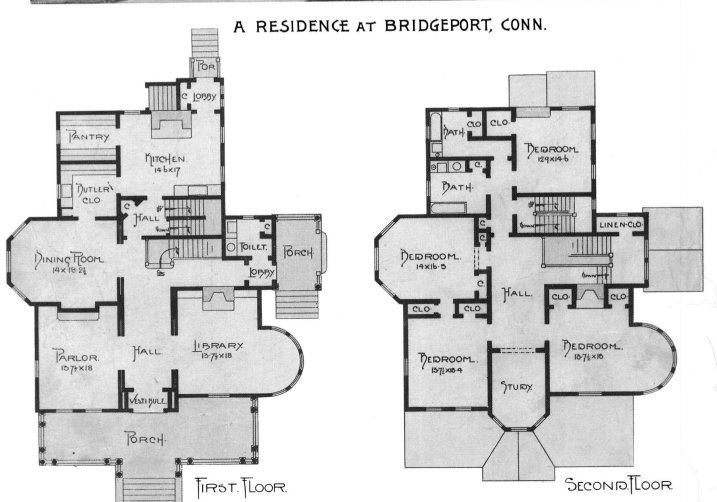

FIRST FLOOR.

SECOND FLOOR.

A RESIDENCE ON PARK PLACE, BRIDGEPORT, CONN.

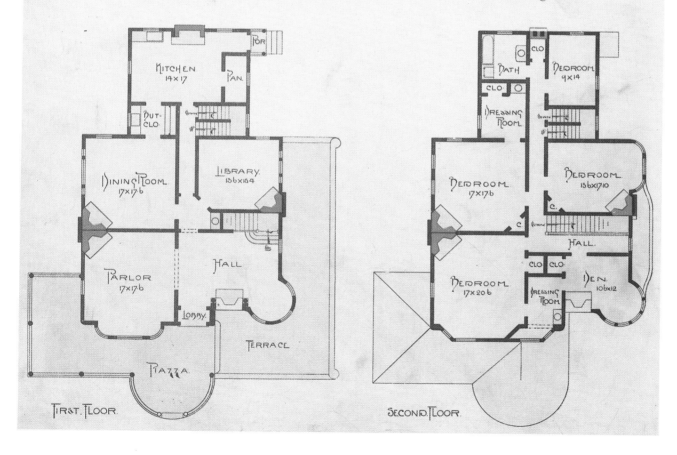

FIRST FLOOR.

SECOND FLOOR.

A RESIDENCE AT PLAINFIELD, N.J.

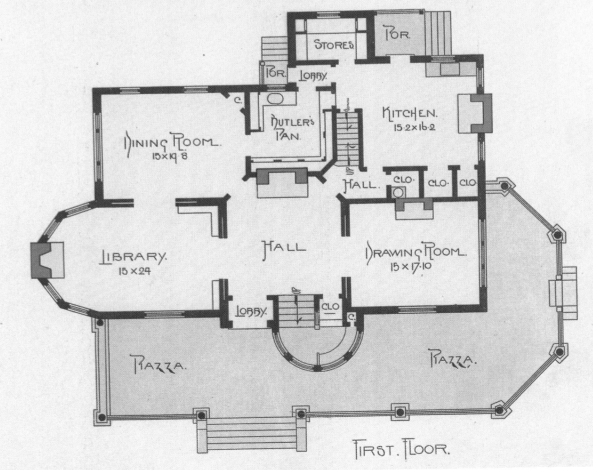

FIRST. FLOOR.

A RESIDENCE AT SPRINGFIELD, MASS.

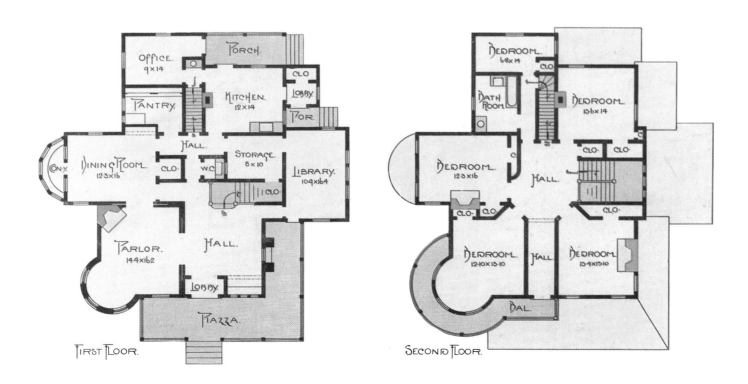

FIRST FLOOR.

SECOND FLOOR.

A RESIDENCE AT SPRINGFIELD, MASS.

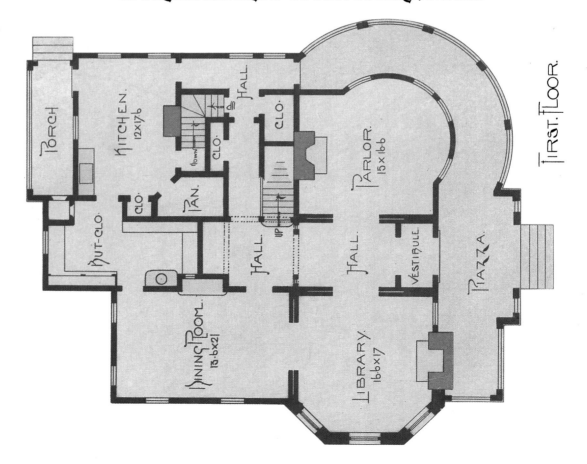

First Floor.

Porch

Kitchen. 12x176

Hall.

Clo.

Clo.

Pan.

Clo.

But-clo.

Hall.

up

Down

Parlor. 15x166

Dining Room. 15·6x21

Hall.

Vestibule.

Piazza.

Library. 166x17

A RESIDENCE AT PELHAM MANOR, N.Y.

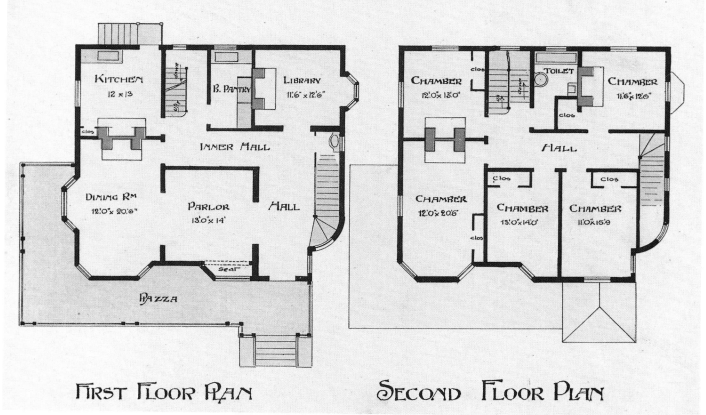

FIRST FLOOR PLAN   SECOND FLOOR PLAN

A HOUSE AT PROVIDENCE, R.I.

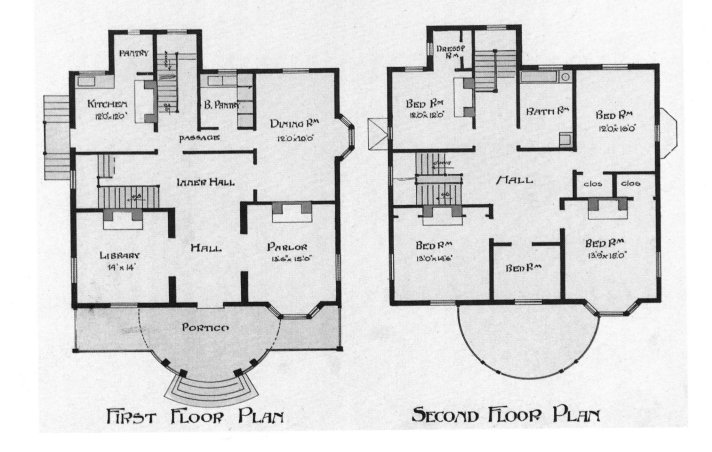

FIRST FLOOR PLAN

SECOND FLOOR PLAN

A RESIDENCE AT EDGEWATER, ILL.

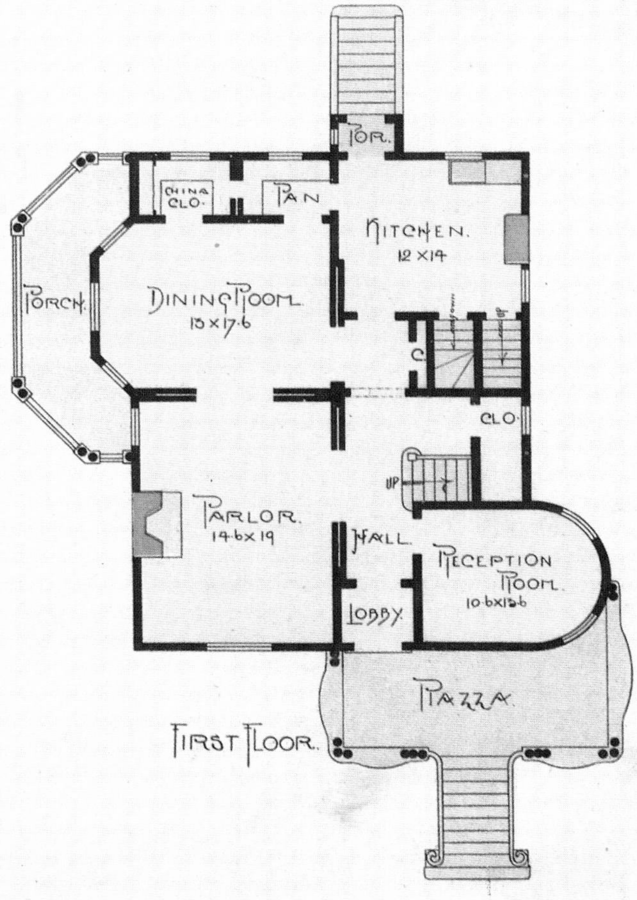

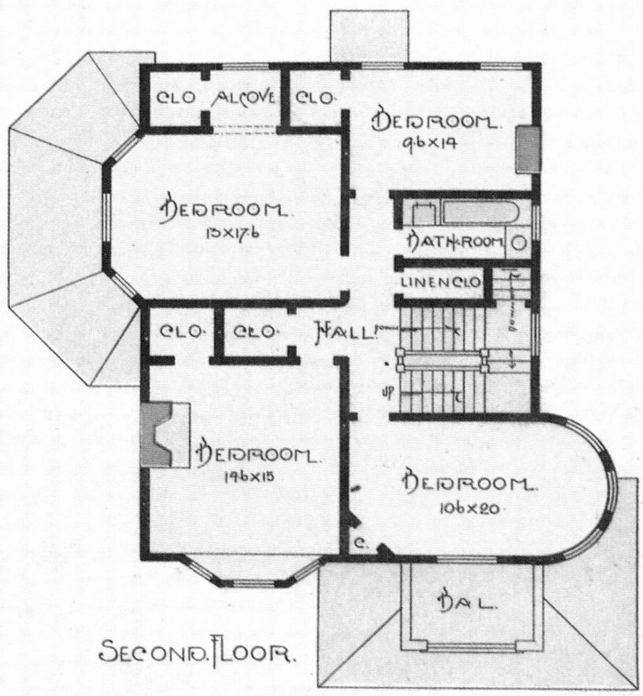

FIRST FLOOR.

SECOND FLOOR.

SCHUMACHER & ETTLINGER, NEW YORK.

Index of Architects

Index of Locations, by State